NEVER
FORGOTTEN

ADVICE FOR ALL GOD'S CHILDREN

NEVER
FORGOTTEN

ADVICE FOR ALL GOD'S CHILDREN

DR. NICKU KYUNGU MORDI

TATE PUBLISHING
AND ENTERPRISES, LLC

Published by Tate Publishing & Enterprises, LLC
127 E. Trade Center Terrace | Mustang, Oklahoma 73064 USA
1.888.361.9473 | www.tatepublishing.com

Tate Publishing is committed to excellence in the publishing industry. The company reflects the philosophy established by the founders, based on Psalm 68:11,
"The Lord gave the word and great was the company of those who published it."

Book design copyright © 2012 by Tate Publishing, LLC. All rights reserved.
Cover design by Kenna Davis
Interior design by Nathan Harmony

Published in the United States of America

ISBN: 978-1-61862-812-1
1. Religion / Christian Life / Spiritual Growth
2. Religion / Christian Ministry / Missions
12.05.07

DEDICATION

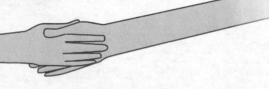

This book is dedicated to God our Father, to Jesus Christ our Savior and Redeemer, and to the Holy Spirit our Comforter in whom we live, move, and have our being. To this Holy Trinity I give all glory and honor for bringing me thus far.

ACKNOWLEDGMENTS

First of all, I wish to thank God, who is the source and the center of all that I do. Without His strength and grace, this book could not have been written.

Secondly, I want to thank my experienced manuscript editor Tertia D. Kaul for working hard to prepare this work to be sent to the publishers. My faithful friend and supporter Dada Mary Nasibi, who has given support for this book to be written. Mary, your dedication is appreciated.

To my husband and prayer partner, George N. Mordi, my children, Bupe Easther and Edith Ifeanyichuku who have allowed me to go into all the world to share God's love with others.

Also, my prayer partners around the world who stand with me to fulfill God's vision and mandate upon my life, especially Helen Asirifi and Pastor Abtow Kabede, Chris and Allyn Saah, Joel and Beth Cornelius, Rev. Devon and Pat Brown, Rev. Rodney Veney, Victor Adomako, Janet Getz. To the advisory board Rev. Hanfere Aligaz, Dr. Loray Blair-Britt, Bishop Agbeja, Bishop Johnson, Pastor Seth Akyea,

Pastor Kwasi Gyimah, Pastor Ghandi Olaoye, Pastor Bayo Adeyokunnu and the I GO/AFJ Leadership Team worldwide and my family of the late Evangelist Joel Kyungu Mwakasege and Anganile Tusekelege Mwaitwalile. I love you all very much and thank God for you.

TABLE OF CONTENTS

INTRODUCTION

In order for you to know your rights in any situation, you have to spend time studying, asking, and listening to more experienced people or those who brought you into this world. It is the duty of parents to teach their children how to live and behave. What we learn when we are young is carried to maturity. We are a product of our environment and associations.

The objective of this book is to remind you and bring to your memory how important and how special you are before God, your other parent, just in case you did not have good parents. With God, however, nothing matters more than *you*. You are God's masterpiece, and you must start believing what God says about *you*. The reason God created you and has kept you alive until today is because He has a plan and a purpose for your life—a special mission and vocation for you to fulfill. The Bible says: "For we are his workmanship, created in Christ Jesus unto good works" (Ephesians 2:10). Even if your position today seems far from your life's purpose, I want to encourage you, you are never forgotten because you are a child of God.

YOU ARE BETTER THAN...

Although you were born or came out of two people, they were just a channel of entry to this world. You are more than just a human being, you are more than male or female, and you are more than the color of your skin. You are even far more than what society or the status quo has labeled you to be. Your worth is beyond the profession you have or don't have; it is even beyond the material things people are measured by—money, cars, houses. You are more than any material thing because in the entire world there is no one like you.

This is very important for you to understand—try never to forget how important and how special you are. Even if you do not feel special at the moment, by faith believe, because it is true. This is your time to forget the past that might have been bad or unfulfilling and reach for God's best for you. You are a child of God and are created in His image for a higher purpose. You are a spiritual being who lives in a body. Your body is temporary. Your body will die one day. Your spirit, however, will live eternally. You came to this world because God has a good plan for you and He wants to fulfill that plan for you as long as you are ready to believe He has not forgotten you.

You are able to read this book because your life is preserved by God, who is your Father. What you are today is a product of many things. Even the language you speak or the food you like to eat is influenced by the culture you were brought up in or where you live. Since you are a spirit being and your spirit will live forever—longer than your physical being—it will be important for you to know and develop the language your Father, the originator of your being, uses.

Unfortunately, many people spend time, money, and whatever they have to pamper the physical being that is temporary. In this book, I want you to really know in your mind and in your spirit so that you will never forget how special you are. I want you to develop and improve your relationship with God, who created you. To improve this relationship, you must spend time with God and talk with Him, and you will come to know that God will never forget you. Isaiah 49:15-16 says, "Can a woman forget her sucking child, that she should not have compassion on the son of her womb? yea, they may forget, yet will I not forget thee. Behold, I have graven thee upon the palms of my hands;"

When I was growing up in my parents' home, I never worried what I was going to eat or wear; everything was provided. When I grew up, I was still in my parents' home, and in order to continue to enjoy all the privileges, I was given some responsibilities and had to live according to their rules. In the mornings, I had to sweep outside with a long sticky broom, wash dishes, and sometimes go to the river to fetch water or wash clothes. Once in a while, when I refused to do what they told me, I got punished. I recall when I refused to go to the river because of friends. My mother did not shout at me, so I thought I was okay. In the evening the meal was rice and meat (this was a special occasion), and I was looking forward to eating. When Mom called us to eat, she calmly took me aside and handed me raw rice and some raw beans, saying, "You did not fetch water, so we did not have water to cook your potion." I cried and tried to convince her that next time I would do anything she wanted me to do. She was firm, and I slept hungry while others enjoyed the meal. From that day, I did everything I was told.

Likewise, God your Father wants you to enjoy all that He has created and given to you pertaining to life and godliness, but you have a part to play by learning how to communicate or how to talk to Him, not only when you are in need. You should talk with Him because you have a relationship with Him. Even when you forget to talk with Him or you disobey Him, you can know you are never forgotten no matter what is happening around you.

HOW TO TALK WITH GOD

To talk to God, we often use the terms *prayer* and meditation. Whatever term makes sense to you, the meaning is the same: talking to God. We all understand—or we hear people say—that prayer is a master key, especially in the Christian circle. That is because prayer connects you to God, who is the Creator of everything, and there is nothing too hard for Him to do. As His child, you also must connect with Him by speaking with Him in prayer. Prayer is part of our being human. For most of us, we use prayer in a religious mode that requires specific formulae or regulations.

For the children of God, especially for those who love to pray, I want to add another dimension that will make prayer a lifestyle and not an activity or a ritual. It is what I call "relational prayer of intimacy." This kind of prayer will cause you to remember how special you are. To develop conversational relationship with God, you will realize you are never forgotten even when you face different challenges of life. In fact, the more you speak with Him, the more you will learn to hear Him with your spirit. For instance, when you are facing challenges, listen to your spirit. I know you can easily hear God say to you, "Do not worry about how to handle this or that. You are my child and I know how to solve your problems." Learning to hear and to obey what God tells you is a foundation for every person who desires to live a joyful and victorious life.

CONSIDER A FOUNDATION

Look at the buildings around you, there is an important aspect you do not see with your physical eyes, and that is the foundation. In life or in marriage, the foundation is vital. A foundation can determine how solid the building or marriage is and how long it will last. If the foundation is weak or poor, ruin or abandonment is inevitable. If the foundation is good, no matter the harshness encountered, it will stand. Likewise for a child of God, regardless of your background or the circumstances you face, you are never forgotten, because your foundation is in your Father, who is God the Creator. He is able to help you in any storm of life.

In Luke 6:48-49, Jesus talked about two people who faced the same storms of life. One of them was able to overcome, while the other was consumed by the storms. The difference between these two was their foundation. He gave an explanation of a person who obeys His Word to be victorious in life. Such a person is:

Like a man which built a house and dug deep, and laid the foundation on a rock: and when the flood arose, the stream beat vehemently upon that house, and could not shake it: for it was founded upon a rock. But a person who hears and does not obey is not victorious. But he that heareth, and doeth not, is like a man that without a foundation built an house upon the earth; against which the stream did *beat* vehemently, and immediately it fell; and the ruin of that house was great.

Luke 6:48-49

It is vital for you, as a child of God, to examine your spiritual foundation in order to enjoy the remainder of your Christian journey. Always remember, you are never forgotten. No matter the hardship or whatever is happening in you or around you, you will be able to stand and overcome because the joy of the Lord can be your strength (Nehemiah 8:10).

Many people have overcome their struggles and problems because of their faith in God. Let me share what happened when I was a young girl. One day, God told me to resign from my good job with the American Embassy in Tanzania and go to Northern Europe as a missionary/evangelist. I felt that was very foolish, even if it was God. I really did not know or understand what He was talking about. "Going to Europe!" This was impossible, and I ignored.

However, as months passed by, I kept on sensing in my spirit God wanted me to do something unusual, but nothing made sense. So I forgot the idea until when I was speaking at a school rally, God showed me exactly where to go—Sweden! And He gave me three months to leave my country. Although it sounded crazy and I had no idea where Sweden was, I knew God had spoken.

I started asking for prayer and direction from my church family and friends; they all thought it was impossible. They said many things out of concern to discourage me that I did not hear from God. My elder sister, though she was in Italy, I felt she also joined their thoughts when she said, "No African girl has ever gone to Europe as a missionary? Where did you get this crazy idea that God wants you to go to Sweden? Who do you think you are?" Indeed, all they said was true, but the more they discouraged me, the more I kept on obeying God and was ready to leave everything to go where He wanted me to go. Yes, they were my family and people I respected, but my relationship with God did not depend on the approval of others. There are times when you know what you hear is non-negotiable; it comes out of a personal relationship with Him as a Father who speaks to you as His child who is loved and who is very special.

Though it was very hard, I knew to obey God was the best for me. At a very young age, I left my very comfortable life, my loving family, my house, my car, my prestigious job—everything I was comfortable and familiar with—to go to the unknown and unfamiliar. God's ways are not our ways. We have to learn to trust and obey Him in every situation. Listen to the words of a man who did not depend on earthly possessions or put his confidence in material things,

> Although the fig tree shall not blossom, neither shall fruit be in the vines; the labour of the olive shall fail, and the fields shall yield no meat; the flock shall be cut off from the fold, and there shall be no herd in the stalls: Yet I will rejoice in the LORD, I will joy in the God of my salvation. The LORD God is my strength, and he will make my feet like hinds' feet, and he will make me to walk upon mine high places.

> Habakkuk 3:17-19

Another one said,

> I will greatly rejoice in the LORD, my soul shall be joyful in my God; for he hath clothed me with the garments of salvation, he hath covered me with the robe of righteousness, as a bridegroom decketh Himself with ornaments, and as a bride adorneth herself with her jewels.

> Isaiah 61:10

Child of God, may the scriptures above encourage you to know you are never forgotten. As I mentioned, going to Sweden meant to leave all without knowing where I was going. I was a young girl in my twenties. No one believed I was obeying God because in those days, it was unusual for an African girl to travel to Europe as a missionary. Missionaries were known to be going to Africa, not the other way around. Above all, to leave without any personal contact of where you were going or church support to back you up seemed a very crazy and unwise thing to do. Nevertheless, I knew I heard from God, who created me and had a higher purpose for my life that I could not comprehend.

By faith I left Tanzania without enough ticket money or any contacts. Before I left, however, I asked God to allow me to stop in Nairobi to talk with a pastor friend and to stop in Milan to ask my sister for the remainder of the airfare as well as to say farewell in case I died where I was going. As I took the step of faith, God's hand was being manifested in every step of the journey. Although it was not easy, I was able to overcome all the obstacles I faced because I knew I heard God and He was in control. This knowing comes when you learn to value your personal relationship with Him more than anything. You enjoy spending quality or intimate time with Him until He can share or speak to you in a way no one can understand but you. What He says to you sometimes might not make sense, but you obey because you know He is your Father who loves you. Whatever He says or does is for your good. The Bible says, "The LORD will not forsake His people, for His great name's sake, because it has pleased the LORD to make you" (1 Samuel 12:22-24).

INTIMACY WITH GOD IS KEY

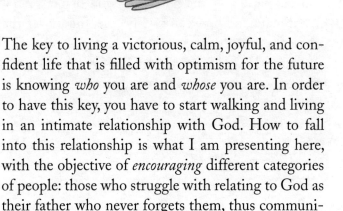

The key to living a victorious, calm, joyful, and confident life that is filled with optimism for the future is knowing *who* you are and *whose* you are. In order to have this key, you have to start walking and living in an intimate relationship with God. How to fall into this relationship is what I am presenting here, with the objective of *encouraging* different categories of people: those who struggle with relating to God as their father who never forgets them, thus communicating with Him in their prayer lives as father is hard; *awakening* those who no longer see the need to pray because they have given up; *uplifting* those who pray the hardest and nothing seems to change for them; and *inspiring* those who do not know how to communicate with God in relational prayers.

No matter where you are or what category you fit into regarding your relationship to communicate with your Father through prayer, I hope that after you finish this book, your attitude toward praying will change, you will actually *enjoy* praying, and prayer will become a lifestyle, not a ministry or a ritual. You will find yourself praying without ceasing (1 Thessalonians 5:17), which means your heart will always be in tune with God and open to His voice, and out of you shall flow rivers of living water (John 7:37-38), which means your words will be filled with life and faith to encourage, inspire, and motivate others. In this book, I want you to understand that I am talking about the relational kind of prayer that is intimate and between two people, the prayer that causes one to pray spontaneously anywhere and at any time. Prayer that will give you joy to always find an opportunity to be with your Father.

THE EFFECT OF PRAYER

For Christians, prayer is what connects us to God. As we pray, we get instructions from Him on how to face personal situations or situations concerning our loved ones, our communities, or even our nation. You might be aware that prayers are going on across the world almost every second, every minute, and every hour of the day around the clock. Prayers have made an impact throughout history. Prayers have changed lives and prayers have changed the course of nations. Prayer is a weapon that is available for every person to use anytime and anywhere. Not just any kind of prayer, but consistent prayers of faith that are done according to His word.

Imagine, if any human being can have access to God through the right kind of prayer, you should be encouraged to develop an attitude of speaking with Him all the time. Be eager to approach Him without fear because you know He is your Father, who never leaves you and you are never forgotten. His door is wide open for you to enter and commune with Him anytime through prayer.

NOT YOUR QUALIFICATIONS

Maybe you are like those who feel they are not qualified to enter into God's presence or to approach
Him because you feel unworthy. I have met people
who have told me, "You are lucky because you know
how to pray and your prayers get answered." I have
to encourage them and teach that prayer is nothing
more than talking. If they know how to talk to their
friends or loved ones, they can also talk to God. At
the same time, I have to say not all my prayers have
been answered, but that does not stop me from talking to Him all the time. Moreover, to feel unworthy is the right position in order to really understand
that God is the one who qualifies you. When you
feel unworthy, you are the best candidate to receive
everything you need as long as you have a desire in
your mind and spirit to connect with God. Even if
you do not say a word, God sees your inner being and
His spirit will help your spirit to pray. The Bible says,

"Likewise the Spirit also helpeth our infirmities: for we know not what we should pray for as
we ought; but the Spirit itself maketh intercession
for us with groaning; which cannot be uttered. And
He that searcheth the hearts knoweth what is the
mind of the Spirit, because he maketh intercession
for the saints (for you) according to the will of God"
(Romans 8:26-27).

Indeed, in ourselves, no one knows how to pray and
no one is worthy to approach God because through
Adam we sinned; we abused all the freedom and the

privileges God intended for us to have in the garden of Eden (Genesis 1:26). When Adam sinned, he was separated from God and was thrown out of God's garden—a place where everything was provided for Him to eat and enjoy; he was thrown out to start working hard to take care of Himself and his wife.

God gave Adam the assignment to till the land and take dominion. In other words, Adam was to be the ruler in the garden of God and enjoy all that had already been created. Everything pertaining to life and godliness was provided for them, but when Adam disobeyed God, he and his wife, Eve, were sent away from God's fellowship and provision. They had to start working hard for everything they needed (Genesis 3:23-24). Although God sent them away from the abundance of everything to a place of want and emptiness, they were never forgotten. Sin brings separation between God and man, which in turn produces emptiness and unfulfillment in life. "But your iniquities have separated between you and your God, and your sins have hid his face from you, that he will not hear" (Isaiah 59:2).

In the natural as well, sin (disobedience, dishonesty, disrespect, pride, selfishness, etc.) brings separation between societies and families. For example, disobedient children are punished often; at times, they are sent away from their parents' homes if they refuse to live according to the rules set by the parents. For wealthy families, disobedient children may be disinherited until they get their act together! When they start obeying and respecting their parents, the relationship is restored and they are allowed to reclaim their inheritance. If societies or families can be separated, imagine what God can do! He is more than the earthly parents—He is our Creator who knew you and me before we were conceived (Psalm 139:13-16; Jeremiah 1:5).

Even when you disobey Him and you do not value or see the importance of being connected with Him, His desire is for you to get closer so that He can help you in your every need. Although He was angry with Adam's disobedience, He never forgot to provide the best for them. When Adam and Eve left God's garden, they provided for themselves inferior materials to wear; they sewed fig leaves to cover themselves. But God, who never forgets anyone, covered them with coats made with skin (Genesis 3:7, 21). In their disobedience and separation from God, He still provided them with the best fur coats! Not made with human hands, but by God Himself. Be encouraged, wherever you are, whatever you are going through, know that God is just a prayer away. Feel free to talk to Him just as you are talking to someone you love or respect.

Even though sin separated us from God who loves us so much, in our separation, He was busy planning another strategy to restore us. As soon as Adam sinned, God knew his action would separate the entire human race. God started to put His plan together that would bring people back to Himself because of His higher purpose for our lives. His plan to redeem us back was to send His only begotten son, Jesus Christ, to die for us. This includes you and every human being who will believe in Jesus (John 3:16). Listen to what God is telling you. "I have loved you with an everlasting love; I have drawn you with loving-kindness" (Jeremiah 31:3, NIV). "While you were in sin, Christ died for you" (Romans 5:8, NIV).

Jesus died for me and for you! He paid a price we cannot fathom, and this has qualified you. "God, who is rich in mercy, for His great love wherewith He loved us, Even when we were dead in sins, hath quickened us together with Christ."

"For by grace are ye saved through faith; and that not of yourselves: it is the gift of God: Not of works, lest any man should boast" (Ephesians 2:4-5; 8-9).

Because of the great price Jesus paid for you, you are qualified to approach God anytime and anywhere. There is nothing in you that qualifies you except the blood of Jesus. "For Christ also hath once suffered for sins, the just for the unjust, that he might bring us to God" (1 Peter 3:18). It is up to you to believe. By faith connect with your Father by developing free communication with Him. Desire to know Him in a deeper relationship as you learn to commune and connect with Him.

HOW TO CONNECT

Twenty-first-century technologies have made it easy for people to connect throughout the world. There are all kinds of ways to connect—first it was tele-grams, then ordinary telephones, now there are cell phones, internet, YouTube, e-mail, Facebook, Twitter, etc. People are constantly connecting with their significant others around the clock through cyberspace. God is more than your significant other. He is our all in all, and whatever we lack He is. He is Spirit who says, "I AM THAT I AM." What you are not, He is, and this is why it is so vital to be connected. *How do we connect with the spiritual being or person within us?* Believe it or not, you have to try to ask yourself this question and then answer it in order not to forget, you are a spirit being and need to connect and *feed* your spirit through proper methods.

Connecting to your spirit requires a method of spiritual intimacy—a deep relationship through what I call the "intimacy relational prayer." This is one kind of prayer that is not emphasized much. As I have travelled to minister and speak to different denominations and ministries around the world and been involved in different prayer conferences and prayer organizations, I have noticed many Christians understand and talk about devotional prayers, warfare prayers, congregational prayers, repentance and intercessory prayers, the individual prayers we request when we are going through hard times, thanksgiving prayers for what God has done, and so on. Indeed, we thank God for all these different kinds of prayers.

The intimacy relational prayer, however, is the foundational prayer that is fundamental to victorious living and contentment in life. This prayer also demonstrates a level of maturity in one's Christian walk or background. How the relationship has developed through the years and the fellowship that has been built between the two. It is a prayer life that is personal and private. In the Bible, Jesus Christ said, "Abide in me, and I in you. As the branch cannot bear fruit of itself, except it abide in the vine; no more can ye, except ye abide in me" (John 15:4). To abide in Christ is personal connection and if it is properly done, it will produce good fruit—good behavior, good attitude, unselfishness, helpfulness, and optimism in life. This is where I want you and me to be.

BEING INTIMATE

Prayer requires speaking, talking, or at times, just being there with someone. For better explanation, let me take your imagination to someone special, be it a friend, spouse, or parents. Think about any person you enjoy spending time with. You can sit or talk for hours without being tired. You can even become intimate by touching or sitting closer to each other while you talk, eat or walk alongside each other. Because you love that person, your time together is special. The Bible speaks on what the children of Israel were told, "And thou shall love the LORD thy God with all thine heart, and with all thy soul, and with all thy might" (Deuteronomy 6:5). This still applies to all of us.

In the New Testament, Jesus was asked by a lawyer which one was the greatest commandment. Jesus replied by quoting the same thing: "You shall love the LORD your God with all your heart, with all your soul, and with all your mind" (Matthew 22:35-37, NKJV).

This intimate kind of love requires your heart, your soul, your strength, and your entire body to be involved in whatever you are doing. This means you have to pay 100 percent attention to your significant other. How much more God who has promised never to leave or to forsake you all the days of your life! To be simple, it is the kind of burning love that is pure and without pretense. Imagine that you are in love with someone special. You cannot wait to get married! When the wedding ceremony ends, you cannot wait to get away for your honeymoon. You go away from everyone and everything else. In your mind, you have forgotten all troubles and your focus is on your being alone with your partner. That moment is very private; it is a moment for the two of you—a holy moment.

My wedding night, however, was not as I have stated above. I did not want to be alone with my husband because I was naïve and ignorant of what the Word of God said. In my mind, I did not want to defile the temple of the Living God—which I was— by being intimate with a man (1 Corinthians 3:16-17). I had all kinds of excuses why we could not make love. It took two days, but I was still very reluctant and sad. It took prayer for my mind to be transformed and the

Never Forgotten

Spirit to assure me it was okay for me to start enjoying my husband and to be relaxed in bed.

It was that time when I understood why the Bible says the bed is holy. Marriage is honorable in all, and the bed undefiled (Hebrews 13:4). The principle of loving God with all your heart and your entire mind is synonymous with sexual intercourse. You are passionate; you concentrate without interruptions in order to enjoy your lover. My objective in this book is to take you to where the love for God is real intimate—where your love for Him is passionate and enjoyable because you know God's love for you is real. The Bible says:

> But God commendeth his love towards us, in that, while we were yet sinners, Christ died for us. That Christ may dwell in your hearts by faith; that ye, being rooted and grounded in love May be able to comprehend with all saints what is the breadth, and length, and depth, and height; and to know the love of Christ, which passeth knowledge, that ye might be filled with all the fullness of God.
>
> Romans 5:8; Ephesians 3:17-19

The Word of God is filled with scriptures to assure you that you are never forgotten and God wants you to have the best.

Believe in your mind and in your spirit that God longs to have *you* spending time with *Him*. He wants to speak to you, to infuse His power until you are trans-

33

formed to His image. He purposed in Himself to create you because He wants to share His love with you. Solomon's Song 7:10 says, "I am my beloved's, and his desire is toward me." God's desire is toward you. Even when you mess up, He does not see or focus on your mess. God looks at you through the blood of His beloved Son, and He continues to love you according to His good pleasure (Ephesians 1:5, 9; Revelation 4:11).

What a Father! He wants you to know and believe His Word that you are never forsaken. No matter what you are going through at this very moment, talk to Him in your mind and in your spirit and tell Him your needs; He will answer and give you peace to hope for the best. Even if everything is going right for you, you are the best candidate to be more intimate with Him because of His faithfulness to you. Take quality time to appreciate Him, because He has not forgotten you. Whatever you have is because of His grace upon your life. Deuteronomy 8:17-18 should be a reminder that God is at work in your life regardless of your position in life or your circumstances.

IS THIS POSSIBLE?

If we look to ourselves, the unpleasant or unfortunate situations in our lives, and what is going on in our nations and the world at large, life will be hard and unbearable. But we do not have to look to ourselves. We have Jesus as our High Priest who loves us. In fact, He loved us so much that He came to live among us as an example of how we should live. He went through so much with people—even with His disciples—but He was focused on the mission He was born to accomplish. On top of that, He willingly allowed Himself to be despised, accused wrongly, ridiculed and finally, crucified. His precious blood was shed. He gave His life so that you might be reconciled back to God (Romans 5:8-9; Colossians 1:14-22).

No wonder the beloved disciple John says, "What manner of love the Father hath bestowed upon [or given] us" (1 John 3:1). You can personalize it and say, "What manner [or what kind] of love God has given *me* [say your name or personalize this scripture for yourself]!" What manner of love indeed. This love that God has given you, the high price that God put on you or what He says you deserve cannot be compared to anything. No silver or gold could measure the worth that God put upon your life. You are more precious than diamonds. You are His masterpiece. He wants to pour out His love upon you and into you if you will allow Him. Take time, be still, lie down, and let Him be the lover of your soul. You are much more worthy than anything in this world, regardless of what you think about yourself. Start believing and say over and over to yourself with confidence that you are indeed a masterpiece because God created you. He never created anything bad or inferior. Amen!

PRAYER OF IMPACT

In the previous chapter, I talked about intimacy and how people in love want to spend time together. The time for each other is a priority. Some spend a lot of money to prove how much they love the other person—some can even forsake their family for the other person—sadly for some, this love lasts for only a while. Human love does not guarantee the person will be with you or love you forever. Imagine when one dies. No matter how much they love each other, no one has ever willingly gone inside the grave when his or her lover or partner was being buried. Though human love is shown in many ways, it has limitations. That was not so with Jesus: He willingly faced all kinds of pain; He was accused and wrongfully judged, but He accepted all without causing a scene or without justifying Himself in order to avoid the cross. John 15:13 tells us what Jesus said. "Greater love hath no man than this, that a man lay down his life for his friends". Paul spoke of Him as "our Lord Jesus Christ, Who gave Himself for our sins, that he might deliver us from this present evil world, according to the will of God and our Father" (Galatians 1:3-4).

Do you understand now how important you are? Do you understand why it is vital to develop better spiritual communication skills so that you can enjoy what has already been accomplished by His death on the cross? Scripture says,

> He died for all, that they which live should not henceforth live unto themselves, but unto him which died for them, and rose again. And you, that were sometime alienated and enemies in your mind by wicked works, yet now hath he reconciled in the body of his flesh through death, to present you holy and unblameable and unreproveable in his sight:
>
> 2 Corinthians 5:15;
> Colossians 1:21-22

The only way to overcome the challenges of life is to love spending time with God through His Word; to study and imitate the life of Jesus, how He overcame this world until He completed His mission victoriously by His death on the cross. It will take effort and determination on your part to reach a level that you know you are rooted in the fullness of God, and you are confident in knowing that you are never forsaken because Christ died for you (Ephesians 3:16-19). Jesus was God and Man as He lived in this world. He came to be your example so that you can imitate

Him. But what was His secret to living victoriously? I believe it was His prayer life.

JESUS'S PRAYER LIFE

One thing that is evident—Jesus's prayer life was not like what the disciples were used to seeing among other religious leaders. Jesus prayed and acted differently. He prayed often and at different times. This was His secret. You do not see anywhere in the scriptures that Jesus had a prayer partner. Even the three closest disciples—Peter, John and James, the inner circle of Christ's disciples—did not know when or where He was praying; they were not part of His intimacy relational prayers. This can be your secret as well, to develop a private, intimate relational prayer life with God that no one is invited except you and Him.

When Jesus wanted to talk to His Father, who is also *your* Father, He prayed alone. I believe He talked with His Father all the time, anywhere. He communicated with Him intimately. When He was alone, He talked with emotion and passion; sometimes I imagine Him just being there, feeling the love of His Father after his disciples had been difficult. Once, we are told, Jesus prayed in such agony that some of his veins burst and blood was mixed with sweat (Luke 22:41-44). This agony prayer was just before He was arrested—the time when His disciples could not even pray for Him and one of His disciples, Judas, came with a crowd to betray Jesus with a kiss. Indeed, human love is not guaranteed!

Can you imagine what you would have done if you were betrayed by your friends? What would you do in such a situation? What kind of prayer would you have prayed? Would you have complained and asked, "Why me, Lord? What have I done to deserve this?" These are what I call "complaining prayers." I am sure that I would have complained. (Even now I have grown and am still growing *out* of such prayers.) Are you among the many people who always pray sad prayers that are filled with problems? Jesus's lifestyle of intimacy relational prayers with the Father enabled Him to handle and overcome every situation He faced. Jesus is the One we should strive to follow. "For we have not an high priest which cannot be touched with the feeling of our infirmities; but was in all points tempted like as we are, yet without sin" (Hebrews 4:15).

This passage from Hebrews tells you that you are not alone nor the first person to face pains, problems or betrayal and you will not be the last! What you go through or what you will go through has happened to others! Jesus also went through for you; that is encouraging. The situation that is bothering you, you are not alone. Just know that you are really never forgotten because you have the Father and Son living in you through the Holy Spirit. It is written, "If a man love me, he will keep my words: and my Father will love him, and we will come unto him, and make our abode with him" (John 14:23).

It is up to you to start believing and acting upon this assurance. Jesus did everything for you. He also said, in this world you will encounter hard situations, but be of good cheer, do not be overcome by them, because He has overcome them for you (John 16:33). Today, there is nothing more that He can do again. He did everything on the cross for you and said, "It is finished." The devil, who is trying to destroy your life, has been defeated and his powers are nullified in Jesus's name. Because you know God and you know that you are His child, you have the key to start to change your attitude toward your circumstances and how you live. Let not your heart be troubled. Neither let it be afraid. Start to develop a simple desire to talk to God as your friend and Father who desires to connect with you just the way you are.

WHAT IS YOUR CONNECTION?

Maybe you belong to a church where prayer meetings are vibrant and prayer groups and devotional prayer with families are promoted. You are encouraged to have prayer groups and partners because "where two or three are gathered" or "two are better than one." That is excellent. You are connected with the right people. Technology has made it easy to connect with many prayers online. You can be in your bed in your house, doing other things while you are praying with others in another place. That is powerful. I thank God for every method that promotes prayers.

If, however, these methods are all you depend on for your spiritual growth, you will be missing the opportunity to be intimate with God. Unless you have your own private time before or after the prayer group or prayer line, you cannot fully benefit from what your Father might say to you alone. Too many distractions during prayer time lead to unproductiveness and spiritual immaturity in most people. At times, even those powerful prayer meetings continue to produce baby Christians.

I am told, people who are struggling to conceive, after the medical doctors have done everything they can, some of them are given a simple advice that has worked. They are told, "When you are making love with your partner, concentrate, focus, and enjoy each other and avoid distractions in your mind." If, medically, it is true that it is important to focus in order to conceive, how much more important is it for us to focus when we talk to the Creator? We have to be focused and connect one hundred percent to God in our spirit in order for His spirit to connect and to be like Him. We have to speak with Him in reverence and awe as we totally surrender to Him and His embrace! If that is your desire, I know God will fill you with Himself. Once He does that, your walk, speech, and perspective in life will be different because you will know your rights in this life.

The Bible says, "Now we have received, not the spirit of the world, but the spirit which is of God; that we might know the things that are freely given to us of God" (1 Corinthians 2:12). When you are connecting with God, it is the spirit of God revealing to your spirit to know without any doubt how prosperous you are, how much you are loved, and how important you are to Him. Third John 2 says, "Beloved, I wish above all things that thou mayest prosper and be in health, even as thy soul prospereth." No one has to convince you; no one has to remind you but yourself. You are the one to decide when you want to spend time to talk with Him and hear more secrets and good news your Father has for you.

The subject of intimacy relational prayer, however, is barely taught in some churches and prayer groups. Those who lack this foundational prayer life find themselves praying problem-solving prayers, focusing mind and heart on problems or unpleasant issues like financial situations, sicknesses, problems with the children or coworkers, the attitude of their boss, career changes, school examinations, and feuds with the family or with church members. Hours, days, and even months are spent asking God to intervene in unpleasant situations. Try to evaluate your own prayer life. How do you pray? Or what do you often hear when others pray? Is too much time spent on problem-solving prayers? Talking more of what the devil is doing rather than what Christ has done!

If we compared the amount of time we spend praying as individuals in different groups, as a nation in different prayer conferences or intercessory prayer walk, can we honestly say we are effective? Look around you; the moral decay is frightening! Or when you listen to the news, who do people listen to or pay attention to more—a person who says, "I am a

Christian," or a person who says, "I am a terrorist"? The attention and fear will go to the terrorist person because of the destructive nature he represents. The goal is to kill and to destroy, and everyone should fear them and pray that they will be changed.

Now, what is the reaction when a person says, "I am a Christian?" What is the general attitude toward Christians? Christians, as people of peace and righteousness, should receive far more respect around the world. We are people who represent the King of kings and the Prince of Peace. However, the opposite is true; oftentimes, as Christians travel around the world, they are subjected to some humiliation just like others. Evil has caused people to fear and be suspicious of each other. The world desperately needs righteous people. Sin abounds more now than ever before. It is time for God-fearing men and women to arise and shine until righteousness covers every community we live in.

I often wonder about this: the more churches fast and pray, the more it seems sin continues to gain ground. For example, in Washington D.C., homosexuals gained ground where prayers were held by all kinds of people and all different groups. Have you ever thought why good people spend time praying and the results are minimal or their praying seems to have little impact? What is happening to us? As children of God, are we advancing His kingdom agenda effectively and wisely? If you are honest, you will say we could do much better.

I believe disunity of the Body of Christ is one factor. Before, I used to attend every prayer meeting that focused on 2 Chronicles 7:14 and 1 Timothy 2:1-5, hoping that one day we would all unite and pray together for one cause. Unfortunately, I discovered no group or denomination paid any attention to the importance of real *unity* of the body except for same-interest unity. I believe it is an oversight that no one wants to take time and effort to unite with other parts of the body that might be different! I am talking this way because the body of Christ is forgetting the power they have. Jesus gave us the secret to empower society and the whole world, but the devil is using what we know and what we say by causing division in different levels.

True unity of the Body of Christ, not uniformity, will bring the glory of God, and many will know Him (John 17:21-23). I believe we can be united for a cause, and it can be done; let us forget all our differences and one day purpose to be voices to transform everything for His glory. God is the only one who loves everyone, and His children are His representatives on earth. He wants us to be instruments to bring many to Him because He does not want anyone to be lost (2 Peter 3:9). If we are united in our diversity for a specific purpose, to demonstrate His love to all people, respect will come to the Body of Christ in a greater capacity that has never been seen before.

Of course, there are a few exceptional voices that God has used to shake nations throughout history.

Even today there are people of God who are respected and admired. There are groups here and there who strive for end time move; thank God for them. My desire is for the entire body of Christ anywhere they are to be respected and be used to bring good change in every aspect of life and society. I want us all to be respected rather than to be despised. God still uses prayers to transform communities and nations. There are times prayers have changed situations instantly. I am also aware that, at times, prayer does not seem to be answered because it is not God's time.

However, here I am talking of changes that we, as God's people, are to affect in communities, societies, as well as in the policies of nations to stand against sin and injustice. Christians are to be respected, not because of their positional influence or the material wealth they have acquired through the years, but because they are Christians and they have a relationship with Jehovah the Creator. Children of presidents or influential leaders are respected in most nations. How much more for the children of God? In addition, too many Christians are not using their God-given opportunities and abilities to share the agape love of Christ with the hurting people and to awaken those who still do not depend on Him, especially national leaders and people in authority. In the Old Testament, they were bold:

> Jehoshaphat...went...among the people... and brought them back to the Lord...Then

he set judges in the land…and said to the
judges, "Take heed to what you are doing, for
you do not judge for man but for the LORD,
who *is* with you in the judgment."

2 Chronicles 19: 4-6 (NKJV)

Be wise now therefore, O you kings [presi-
dents] be instructed, you judges of the earth.
Serve the LORD with fear, and rejoice with
trembling.

Psalm 2:10-11

Christians are to be a voice that can bring solutions
to challenging problems that face individuals, families, communities, and nations. Our Father expects
His children to be a voice to turn situations around
in our world. You can start by totally depending on
His instructions and His grace to guide you through
as you purpose to live and love for Him. Once you
know His love for you is everlasting you will start
loving others without struggle. Your life will change
and you will be free to let others know they are loved,
forgiven, and never forgotten.

HOW TO MOVE FORWARD

What I am about to say does not reflect all prayers, but some personal prayers that have not been answered because of what we say after the prayers. We spend hours praying, telling God what we are going through and by faith we confess that He will answer. Yet, as soon as we finish, we start talking the opposite of what we have confessed or prayed. In so doing, we nullify our prayers with our own words of doubt. The Bible warns against vain speaking or talking words that have no faith.

"He that will love life, and see good days, let Him refrain his tongue from evil, and his lips that they speak no guile" (1 Peter 3:10). "If any man among you seem to be religious, and bridleth not his tongue… this man's religion is vain" (James 1:26). "Whoso keepeth his mouth and his tongue keepeth his soul from troubles (Proverbs 21:23).

I will share some examples of how God has answered some prayers without people struggling. As a child of God, created in His image, you are a spirit being; therefore, how you think and what you speak determines the results you get. This is important to take into account for victorious living.

Let us focus more on an individual quality of prayer that produces results, the intimate relational prayer I spoke about earlier in this book. I intend to help some of the good prayer warriors avoid ritualistic or circumstantial prayers. These are the prayers we do because we are in a prayer ministry or the prayers that arise because of what is going on or what we want to happen with others. Then there are the emergency prayers, which require us to panic and call several people to pray. Once in a while, these kinds of prayers are all right—and they *will* happen. For the children of God, however, prayers are not ritualistic or circumstantial; they flow out of the relationship that we have built with Him—where prayers become relational rather than a duty or ministerial.

I do not know if it is my own observation or if you have experienced the same, but it seems that, often, some of the people who are intercessors or those who are in prayer ministries are faced with all kinds of issues or problems. We often hear that they are facing problems because of their prayer life and that they are easy targets for the enemy. In some cases, that is true; the enemy will target those who have totally committed everything to the Lordship of Christ. For some, however, this is only an excuse for the real issues that go on in their lives. Some of them do not take time to study and know the Word of God in order to pray aright. Jesus said,

> Come unto me, all ye that labour and are
> heavy laden, and I will give you rest. Take
> my yoke upon you, and learn of me; for I am
> meek and lowly in heart: and ye shall find
> rest unto your souls. For my yoke is easy, and
> my burden is light.
>
> Matthew 11:28-30

To learn of Jesus is to follow in His steps in every aspect of life. To learn how He prayed is to imitate Him. He used few words in public prayers, but He spent a lot of time alone in prayer. This is what we should aim to do—spend more time alone in prayer, not you talking all the time. Sometimes prayer means being still and letting Him talk to you. Jesus's intimacy lifestyle with His Father resulted in a victorious life. No wonder He told His disciples,

> But when ye pray, use not vain repetitions, as
> the heathen do: for they think that they shall be
> heard for their much speaking. Be not ye there-
> fore like unto them: for your Father knoweth
> what things ye have need of, before ye ask him.
>
> Matthew 6:7-8

The Spirit has been telling me to share with the intercessory team and Christians in the Body of Christ to change some of our prayer methods. We must develop a hunger to be close to the heart of God in intimacy prayers; we must desire to spend quality time in isolation. Find a private place to sit, kneel, or lie down and surrender all to Him. If we do this, we are confident that our Father will deal with whatever we are facing or might face. Cultivate a lifestyle of loving and pleasing Him, because He knows what you need before you even speak. The Bible says, "And it shall come to pass, that before they call, I will answer; and while they are yet speaking, I will hear" (Isaiah 65:24). God will hear you even before you speak because you have learnt to be alone with Him through His Word. You can say like Jeremiah 15:16, "Thy words were found, and I did eat them; and thy word was unto me the joy and rejoicing of mine heart: for I am called by thy name, O LORD God of hosts."

Remember the two people I spoke about, who are in love (real love) and what happens when they get married. Their focus is not on their problems or to talk too much; their focus is on enjoying each other. Watch how their hands move from head to toe, touching here and there; their eyes are closed or fixed on each other while the heartbeats become irregular. At that moment, they are pouring their whole hearts, minds, souls, and bodies into each other. Time has no relevance or time passes so quickly when they are with each other.

Even though human intimacy falls short and might last only a few hours before reality hits, no matter how short that moment lasted, the experience brought joy to the lovers. All the tension and frustration disappeared because they were focusing on loving, enjoying, and appreciating each other. This is where I want you to be, to love God with all your heart, with all your soul and with all your might.

BEING INTIMATE WITH GOD

God's love for you is much more than any human love or affection. God is the one you can 100 percent trust in His Word and know He will never forget you or disown you. He will never fall out of love with you and He never gets tired when you want to approach Him. In fact, He invites you to a time of fellowship because He is deeply in love and desires to do anything for you. But even if you are not sure where you stand and how in love you are with Him, His love will never change for you. But assuming you are also deeply in love with Him when you are with Him, you want to hear His heartbeat and His assurance to you, saying, "Fear not, for I have redeemed *you*; I have called you by name, you *are* Mine" (Isaiah 43:1). In such an atmosphere, time will seem to disappear without you knowing because you are enjoying His presence.

Jesus, our perfect example, prayed often and any-where. At times, He spent the whole night praying, talking, and being in His Father's presence (Mark 1:35; 6:46; Luke 6:12; 9:18). After spending time with God, He did not need to contemplate what to do about problems that came up, and neither did He take hours casting, binding, or rebuking. Instead, He just spoke. One day, He even told his disciples that if they had faith as a grain of mustard seed, they could command any problem to be removed, and their words would be effective, "for verily I say unto you, if ye have faith as a grain of mustard seed, ye shall say unto this mountain, Remove hence to yonder place; and it shall remove; and nothing shall be impossible unto you" (Matthew 17:20).

Indeed, the disciples noticed how Jesus handled problems. He was calm and did not panic like they did (Matthew 8:24-26). For three years, they noticed His prayer life was different, so they decided to find out His secrets by saying, "Lord, teach us to pray" (Luke 11:1). I believe the disciples wanted to be effective like their Master. This can happen to anyone who has a desire to grow deeper in faith. You can be more effective than you are now. Just believe and take a step of faith to fall in love with Jesus. Become a radical lover, and many fears and problems will be consumed by His presence.

In Matthew 6:6, when Jesus talks about praying in secret, I believe He was laying a foundation of the intimacy relational prayer. He also talked about closing the door. In order to understand fully, let me take you back to your intimate relationship with your significant other. Imagine, for a moment, how you romantically talked with each other. If you were on the phone, you did not want the conversation to end. Then, when you met, if there were people around, your eyes would communicate with each other without saying a word. You would wait until they left to share your deepest thoughts and emotions with each other. The young lovers of the twenty-first century can relate better to the desire of talking so long on phones, computers, and even staying days in bed while all other things do not matter as much.

Maybe you did not have any experience of a significant other and you cannot relate to what I am saying. Nevertheless, you know there is a longing deep down in your heart to experience love or to be loved. This longing in your heart was created by God, who is the source of your life. He is the foundation of your being. I therefore, encourage you, and I believe you can start experiencing God's love right now. Pause for a moment and tell God, who has never forgotten you, to fill your heart with His love. Be sincere and specific to what you need. Let your feelings and desires be known to Him, and He will answer you. He has promised never to forsake you when you call on Him for help (Psalms 34:4-8; 121:1-2; Isaiah 41:10).

It is the same with God, your Father, who is also the lover of your soul—all of His attributes spell love. When you decide to talk to Him (pray), you should have the same emotions. In fact, it should be a longing for any child of God to spend time talking to God. He is perfect, He is Holy, He is strong, He is powerful, He is lovely and wonderful, and yet He desires to spend quality time in secret with you. What an honor and a privilege to be loved by the Creator! You have to understand that you are a unique person regardless of what position you have or do not have in society or what you might be going through right now, and your background has nothing to do with how God sees you. God looks at you through the finished work of Christ, nothing else.

When you plan to spend more time alone talking with God relationally in prayer, your nature will change. Your burdens will seem to melt like the hills that melt as wax in the presence of God (Psalm 97:5). When you leave His presence after hearing what He has to tell you, you will feel lighter and more joyful. No matter the circumstances, you will see and talk differently; your mouth will be filled with optimism because you see things through His eyes. You will be walking by faith and not by sight (2 Corinthians 5:7). You will start to change and be more like Him.

It is my desire to be more like Him each day. Reflect Him in everything I do. Be utterly consumed with His love to totally give my life for His service. Since that is my desire, I have to purpose each day to surrender and depend upon His grace to lead me on. It is not easy, but it is achievable through Him and through Christ, who has done everything and whose grace operates in me, my new man, through the Holy Spirit. I have spoken on how God through the Holy Spirit told me to leave my family, my country and be a missionary in Sweden. Another time I was preaching in a crusade when two young men asked me to go and preach in their country of Zambia. I told them it was not possible because my schedule did not allow me at that time. I was already going to preach in another city and then return to Sweden to continue the mission work.

Five days after we finished the crusade, I went to get the train ticket for where I was supposed to go. When I reached the ticket counter, I heard the spirit of God say, "Do not go to Mwanza, but go to Zambia as you were requested." The voice was so strong and so clear I had to step aside and talk to the people who were going to go with me. They did not understand and they had not prepared to go somewhere else. They refused to get the tickets or to go with me without any plans. In fact, no one knew where the two boys came from, apart from me telling them what they said. I went to ask the pastor. No one had any information about them and no one could locate them. It was obvious to many that I would not go because it did not make sense.

Because I heard from God, it was my responsibility to change our plans and obey God to go where He wanted me to go. The only thing I knew about the two young men was that they came from Kitwe, Zambia and they could sing. In reality, that was not proper information or address to locate people in a foreign land, but that was what I had. I had to leave for Zambia on a day I was scheduled to go to Mwanza. I left without knowing exactly where I was going. Everyone was concerned because war was going on in Southern Africa. The soldiers of Ian Smith from Northern Rhodesia (now Zimbabwe) were in several parts of Zambia. It would have been the wisest thing to give an excuse why I could not go or why I could not obey God.

Nevertheless, I had to obey God and leave knowing it was not safe. The courage to obey and leave is because I have learnt, through experience and in my intimate relationship with Him, to believe Him even if it does not make sense. Though I did not have names or addresses of where I was going, God gave me enough clue of the city and the country. Isaiah 55:8-9 says, "For my thoughts are not your thoughts, neither are your ways my ways, saith the LORD. For as the heavens are higher than the earth, so are my ways higher than your ways, and my thoughts than your thoughts." This is another reason for this book, to encourage God's children to know their Father through His Word, and to learn to spend quality time in fellowship or in prayer. One word or idea from God can transform your life.

WHAT IS INTIMATE PRAYER?

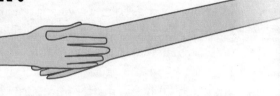

Intimate or relational prayer involves your entire demeanor and your entire being. It is not a struggle or a responsibility you are given to do. Talking to your Father who loves you very much is a time of joy and you look forward to it. It is prayer that carries relational feelings and no one has to remind you to do it except you. You do not shout or yell. You are relaxed, and you are enjoying speaking with Him. At times, you just lie there without speaking a word except you are feeling His embrace and hearing Him speak softly. He may be rebuking you, encouraging you, or giving solutions to handle the problems and cares you have. Whatever the situation, He will be affirming His love as you sit, kneel, stand, or lie and surrender in His presence. You can be walking alone while in fellowship with Him as you feel or sense His presence. He will be there.

I have heard many couples say that when they want something to be done or want to ask for special favors, they make sure the mood is right, *or* they purposefully create the right mood. But God is always the same—yesterday, today, and forever (Hebrews 13:8). It is we who have to cultivate the mood of approaching Him. Better still, we do not have to create any kind of mood as long as we approach Him through Christ. We can speak to Him with the confidence of knowing that Jesus has done all for us through His death on the cross. On your own, you cannot approach God. No matter how hard you try to please God with good works or church rituals, your righteousness is like filthy rags (Isaiah 64:6). What you think is righteousness is not righteousness in God's sight. The only righteousness that He recognizes is through the blood of His Son, Jesus Christ. God made it easy. Jesus did all the work; you just have to enjoy your fellowship with Him as you approach the Father in His name. "And whatsoever you shall ask in my name (Jesus) that will I do, that the Father may be glorified in the Son (John 14:13, 15:16). Another scripture says, "Giving thanks always for all things unto God and the Father in the name of our Lord Jesus Christ" (Ephesians 5:20).

WHAT IS YOUR PERSPECTIVE?

Think for a moment—how do you view God? Do you see Him as a loving Father with His arms wide open to embrace and kiss you no matter what you have done? Or do you see Him as a judge or a Father who is always mean, seeing nothing good in you? No matter where you are or the bad experiences you've had with your biological father, let this book help you see God as your loving Father who cannot be compared with any created being. He is your Father who knows you well and He knows your needs before you even ask (Matthew 6:8). Hear what He says. "If ye then, being evil, know how to give good gifts unto your children, how much more shall your Father which is in heaven give good things to them that ask him?" (Matthew 7:11).

There is a good illustration in the Bible concerning a disobedient child who took all his inheritance against his father's will. He left home and went away to enjoy life (so he thought). While he was away from His father's house, he was away from his provision, from his protection, and from his guidance. He started living without any accountability and in sin—prostitution, gambling, and he wasted all his inheritance. He also lost his joy, his dignity, even his life was being wasted because he could not find food to eat. The devil uses the same deception to deceive many people to think God does not really care as the Word says. He lies by convincing them that they will be better off if they do not obey Him. Whatever feels good, that is what they should do because it is their life.

Many fall into this trap of doubting God's love and care like this prodigal son. They start living outside their Father's will and thus giving room to the devil, who then starts to steal their joy of belonging to a family. He then kills all the relationships to make you feel lonely and unlovable. The mistakes you have done, the devil will magnify them until you feel life is not worth living and you start contemplating suicide. Do not believe anything the devil tells you. He is a liar who wants to destroy you (John 10:10). God will never forget you.

When the prodigal son was wasting away his money and his life, his father never forgot him. Every day he used to look at the window, longing for his return. One day the boy came to his senses. The Bible says, "And he arose, and came to his father. But when he was yet a great way off, his father saw him, and had compassion, and ran, and fell on his neck, and kissed Him" (Luke 15:20).

How did his father see him when he was still far away? I believe the very first day the son left in disobedience to his father's will, the father started longing to have his son back home. His fatherly love for his child never gave up. Be encouraged because God's love for you is much more. Especially if you know your relationship with Him is not all that great! Do not be discouraged; you can start to pray and desire to know Him more and His spirit will perfect your longing for Him.

How you perceive God will determine how you approach Him and how you benefit from all He has freely given you. Because I know He is my father, when I am in trouble or have done what I should not have done and cry for help, I imagine He smiles and says, "That is my silly daughter," and He sends help. Sometimes it takes a long time for help to come, but I still believe and patiently wait in hope because I know He never forgets or forsakes me. If you see Him as your loving Father, in your prayers you will talk normally—in your ordinary voice or ordinary vocabulary without religious jargons or tones. Your prayers will be conversational, emotional, and passionate. Sometimes there will be a moment of joy, laughter, or sorrow—and tears at times—depending on you and your circumstances.

When I hear some people pray while changing their voices and their vocabulary, I wonder if God asks, "Who is this?" God wants us to be real and to approach Him just as we are. He is our Father who knows everything about us. If you are a parent, do you want your children to approach you with different voices or strange vocabularies? I assume even if you have anyone you call friend or family, you will like them to talk and be themselves without pretending or imitating someone else! Yet we seem to think God does not mind the mask we put on in prayer! Whatever perception you have of God, let it be a perception that will cause you to fall in love with Him more than before, and I hope by now you understand a little more of how much you are really loved!

CONSIDER MATTHEW 6:6
Let us consider and ask what Jesus meant when He said, "Enter into your closet." I believe He meant for

us to go to a secret place where we can be *alone* with God. "Close the door" means no one sees you or hears you—you are alone. Some people do not know how to pray alone because they think prayer is to be done by special, qualified persons. These people do not know what prayer truly is. There are others who do not want to be still and hear themselves think. They are surrounded by noise and seem to function better around others. Maybe some of us are afraid to discover who we really are if we remain silent and alone with God. We do not want isolation, and that is why we have to pray with others, have music, or be on the phone, etc. Some of us are our worst enemy; we do not enjoy or take advantage of the now moment. What has made us stagnant, unhappy, depressed, unproductive, or unfruitful are the experiences of our past. May God deliver you right now! You deserve to live an abundant life because you are a child of God.

In an earlier chapter I shared a personal experience that I want to repeat. When I got married in Tulsa, Oklahoma, I gave different excuses why we could not make love. I frustrated my husband and myself because of the past beliefs that were good then but very bad on my wedding night. However, after a few years or so of enjoying being married, I received this revelation of what it means to enter into the closet and close the door. I discovered that the time to make love was *and is* in secret. But it seems our prayers are often surrounded with distractions. It is like when we are ready to be intimate with our partner in the center of our love making, one wants to talk on the phone, read messages, or worse still, one wants love making only in public so that others can see and hear how romantic they are. This is not normal. Yet when it comes to praying, this is what most of us know how to do. We only pray in church, with family, friends, and with prayer partners; we have not learned the intimate relational prayers of being alone with God.

Maturity comes when you know how to enter into the closet, close the door, and then pray to your Father—or talk to your Father—who sees in secret. The time or the place is *not* public. This means what you share with your Father is between you and Him. What you tell Him or He tells you will be demonstrated in your lifestyle. You will produce good fruits that reflect Jesus in words and in deeds, moving those around you to love and to do good works until they give glory to God because of you (Hebrews 10:24; Matthew 5:16).

The meaning of closing the door is "closing your mind." Train your mind to focus on Him *alone*. I know there are times when you pray that your mind is running in different directions; it also happens to me. And when my mind starts wandering, I have to learn to close the door! The devil is always trying to distract you not to have full satisfaction in the presence of your Father God (1 Peter 5:8). This is why it helps to close your eyes when you pray so that your spirit, mind, and soul are connected to one thing—

focusing on talking to the Father. Just like we have talked about being intimate with a person, with every faculty of our being, concentrating and not wanting distractions, this should be even more so when we are alone with God the Creator, who is able to reward us openly. If you operate in this manner, everyone will see you are different; you have reached maturity to know that you are truly a child of God who totally depends on Him. You will be longing to find time when you can enter the closet, close the door, and pray or talk to your Father.

CHARACTERISTICS OF PERSONAL INTIMACY

A lifestyle of personal intimacy is connected with a desire to grow: to behave and act differently. Paul said, "When I was a child, I spake as a child: I understood as a child, I thought as a child: but when I became a man, I put away childish things" (1 Corinthians 13:11).

If you live a lifestyle of personal intimacy, some of the following characteristics will be evident:

- You will live a victorious life

- You will handle situations differently

- Your prayer life will be effortless

- You will be a person of peace and optimism in the midst of storms, just like Jesus was. (Luke 7:22-25)

There are many examples in the Bible to indicate that people who knew who they were had confidence in their faith in God the Father. These people spoke few words or did simple actions that did not make sense, but situations changed. For example, Joshua was faced with an impossible situation, but he did not panic. Instead, he spoke to the sun and the moon to stand still. Both the sun and the moon obeyed Joshua, which means the earth did not rotate; nature obeyed the words of Joshua (Joshua 10:12-14). The Bible says that there was no day like that before or after. That was in the Old Testament when God heard the voice of a man who dared to speak the impossible, and it happened.

As a person in the dispensation of Grace, you are living in a time when the Holy Spirit is ready to work through you, in you, and with you. You can speak and situations can change. At times, it might not make sense to you, but as long as you have heard your Father telling you to speak, obey and speak. This effortless speaking, however, happens when you have developed an intimate relationship with God as your Father.

Let me share other personal experiences that took place in Africa. One day, a young man who was assigned as my driver during a crusade in Dar es Salaam, Tanzania shared how he and his wife had been married for quite a while but had no children. I felt in my spirit to remove the scarf I was wearing and give it to Him for his wife and she would conceive. I did not say anything to Him about how I felt in my spirit, nor did I say I would pray for them; I just kept quiet listening to him. Just before I got out of the car, I took the scarf and said, "Go give this to your wife and you will have a child." I spoke without hesitation, and I did not think about it anymore.

After six years or so, I was having several conferences in the same city. Between the meetings, I was driven to another large church were I was scheduled to speak in their second service. We arrived before the first service was over. We were taken in the bishop's office to wait. After a while, the bishop came into the office to welcome us. But before she entered, one of the pastors who was with the bishop's entourage rushed ahead of them all and jumped to hug me until we both fell on the couch. It was embarrassing and humiliating. Immediately I stood and said to him, "What is all this? You have to explain to me and all these people what this strong hug was for." (Though I spoke with a joking tone, I was very serious. Deep in my mind I was thinking something like, *Who are you to push the guest speaker down in the presence of strangers! What will they think?*

With a big smile, the man said, "You do not remember me. I was your driver during the Big November Crusade in Jangwani. On the last day, I told you about the problems we were having. You did not say much, but you gave me your scarf to give to my wife to wear, and you said we would have children. I took your words very seriously and told my wife what you said. After a few months, my wife conceived. I did not know how to contact you. When

I saw you today, I could not behave myself except to rush to hug you! God used you to answered our prayers, and now we have three children. We were all blessed by the testimony." After hearing him, it was easy for me to explain to my non-Swahili speaking guests who travelled with me. The embarrassment of someone falling on top of me turned into praises. Although I had forgotten him and about what I said, God did not forget.

Another time, I was in Togo, West Africa, speaking at a conference for pastors from French-speaking countries. After the conference, a pastor picked me up to travel to Benin for another meeting. As we were going, the pastor was pointing out to me important sites along the way. When we crossed the border into Benin Republic, we reached the city of Godomey; there he pointed out to me a beautiful monument and said, "Dr. Mordi, you see that monument? It was built to dedicate the country to the ancestors and the voodoo worshippers. The president declared a week of celebration and people came from around the world, including the Pope from Rome."

My spirit was grieved when I heard what he said. I could not believe that in the twenty-first century a government leader was dedicating his nation to idols. At that moment, I reflected on how, in America, God had told me to mobilize Africans and Friends of Africa on the third Saturday of every month to unite and pray for the redemption of nations by "Claiming Africa and America for Jesus." I turned to the pastor and said, "Stop the car. I will lay my hands on the monument and it will fall down." He looked at me with astonishment. "Dr. Mordi," he said, "no one is allowed to go near the monument! There is a big ring surrounding it. Only fetish priests are allowed to enter to offer sacrifices and pour libations and you are not one them,"

I told him, "I will take a picture and lay my hands on it until the monument falls down." He looked at me like I was crazy as he pulled the car off the road. He did not say a word as I took a picture of the monument.

When we arrived at the capital city of Cotonou and went for the meeting, the church was packed. As I was preaching, I kept on talking about the monument and making declarations, without any hesitation or doubt that it would fall. I prophesied about the next election that the president would be a man who would fear God. After I had preached two days in Cotonou and God's power was being manifested in every service, the pastor was convinced to hold another crusade near the monument. He agreed with what I was saying because he saw the power of God performing miracles among the people. I would preach in Cotonou and later drive to Godomey.

Every night, during the crusade outside the mayor's office, many were saved, and God did many miracles of healing and deliverance. Fetish priests and witch doctors brought their charms and quads to be destroyed as they gave their lives to Christ.

Throughout this time, I continued to confess the destruction of that monument, which was built by the government to worship idols instead of the Creator. At the end of the crusade, the pastor could not help but plant a church there to continue to minister and disciple the new converts. The monument, however, was still standing, no matter how much we prayed or stretched our hands for it to fall, but that did not change my confession.

I left the Republic of Benin for another meeting in the country of Ivory Coast. It was my first time to be there, and I did not know anybody. When they delayed to pick me up from the airport, many things went through my mind to make me doubt God, especially since the monument did not fall in Benin! I learnt that instead of dwelling on what did not happen, I had to encourage myself to focus on what God had done. After a while, my host came and I went straight to the revival service. After four days in Abidjan, I returned home. I printed the picture and shared with my church and the prayer team how the monument would fall. I started laying my hands on the picture of the monument and speaking for it to fall. Many did not believe, but that did not stop me from speaking what God had spoken. After a few weeks, I got a call from Benin saying the monument had fallen down. I gave God all the glory for confirming His Word spoken through an ordinary vessel.

LESSON TO LEARN

God is faithful and we must remain faithful to what He has spoken, no matter how unpopular it might be. Precious reader, has God spoken things to you that did not make sense and you forgot about them? Has He spoken things to you that have not yet been fulfilled? Has He spoken things that you are afraid to tell others because they sound crazy and impossible? Keep on believing God; He will bring it to pass. He is your Father who loves you. Even if you have a situation that you have been praying about for a long time, ask your Father what He wants you to do. Don't be surprised if He tells you, "Stop praying. I have heard you. Instead, spend time thanking Me and then speak to your situation—not to Me." He also might answer by asking you, "What do you have?" In order to get a breakthrough or to change the situation that you do not like, you have to use what you have or take action toward your determined goal.

When you spend time with your Father, some of His power through His Word will become part of you. You will internalize until you start to understand why Paul said, "In everything give thanks: for this is the will of God in Christ Jesus concerning you" (1 Thessalonians 5:18). No matter how hard or how terrible the situation might be, know that you are not forgotten. Learn to run to your Father in all your pains or struggles. He is with you and will provide you with His strength to endure (Isaiah 43:2-3a).

Earlier, I spoke on how Jesus taught about having little faith, in fact, as little as a grain of mustard seed (that is *really* small). Imagine that if you have such a tiny bit of faith, Jesus went on to say that you can say to any of your problems or difficulties, "Be removed," and they will be gone (Matthew 17:20). I believe you have far more faith than a tiny grain of mustard seed. Let me explain. When you enter a house or any place where you see a chair, or when you are given a chair to sit, you do not inspect that chair to see if it will support you. When you see a chair or you are given a chair to sit, you do not think anything except to sit because you know it will hold and support you. That is faith. You do many things that require faith and you can learn to apply the same faith concerning God and His Word. When He says to you, "He loves you more than anyone else," believe and smile; you have a great lover. If He tells you, "He will never leave nor forsake you," take it, internalize it, and start acting upon it. Do not let the devil or any person convince you otherwise.

When Jesus says you can speak and it will be gone, indeed it can happen. Remember my examples. I just spoke for them to have a baby, and it happened. It also means even if the situation has not changed, or the problem is still there after you have spoken, you will not let it occupy your mind or let it bother you. You will believe in what you have spoken and leave it to God. Your mind has to be free from problems if you expect to be consumed with loving God, thinking and meditating upon His Word in any situation.

God has all kinds of solutions for whatever you need. Your Father is great, and there is nothing impossible that He will not do for your good as long as you let Him be the center of your life. Try practicing this kind of problem-free mindset: cast all your cares on Him because you are God's child and you are not forgotten. Start sleeping like a baby because your Father never sleeps (Psalm 121:4-8).

Remember the scarf I gave the husband to give to his wife. I did not continue to think about him or their situation. In fact, I forgot even about my scarf. Remember the monument that I declared would fall? There was nothing in me or in the scarf to make the woman get pregnant or anything in me to cause the monument to fall down. It was only that God honored the words He spoke to me and I spoke them out loud. After speaking, I did not fill my mind with unbelief concerning what I had spoken. Though at the time, the words did not make sense; by faith, I obeyed God. This is the faith I wrote about in my autobiography in 1994, *Blind Faith: God's Amazing Miracles* (with foreword by Dr. Oral Roberts).

Do you now understand why I say you have more faith than you give yourself credit for? Your faith has made you do great things like going from one place to another, whether on foot or by car, you left point A believing you would reach point B. This is faith you can use and you have been using. By faith today believe Jesus died so that you can be free, focus on Him and not on your hardships or difficulties. He suffered for you; do not allow your heart, mind, and soul to be filled with problems. Problems will always be part of life, but you can decide to live above them. Try not to listen to popular opinion or to do only what makes sense. Often I am told, "Dr. Mordi, you have to be realistic." Sometimes I even hear, "That does not make sense!" In the natural, it surely does not, but we have to live by faith and not by sight. At times, it is a matter of spiritual maturity; when you hear a word or get an idea from your Father, you leave all reality behind and move in a different dimension that is cultivated in your private moments as you fellowship with Him through His Word. All my life I have loved and walked with Him, yet many times I feel and I know I do not know Him at all and that gives me more desire to know Him like Paul said in Philippians 3:9-14. "And be found in him, not having mine own righteousness, which is of the law, but that which is through the faith of Christ, the righteousness which is of God by faith: That I may know him and the power of his resurrection, and the fellowship of his suffering."

BIBLICAL EXAMPLES

Imagine young David. One day, his father gave Him a simple, ordinary errand to do. He was sent to deliver food to his brothers who were on the front lines of battle with the Philistines. He was a young boy who had never fought in a war. When he arrived at the warfront, he saw a well-trained, well-equipped army in fear of *one* man named Goliath. The army was trained to fight; they had sufficient ammunition for war, but they were intimidated by the size of Goliath and forgot who they were and the potential they had as soldiers. Goliath took advantage of their fear and he kept intimidating the army with his words.

In the New Testament we have a story about a woman who did the unthinkable by taking a simple action that changed her life. The action she took was first conceived in her mind because she was sick of being sick. She was determined to change her situation no matter what method she used. The Bible gives an account that after being sick for twelve years, though she spent all she had on doctors, no one could cure her. She even sold all her belongings just to pay for medical bills. But one day she heard Jesus was passing in the neighborhood. In spite of her weakness, she made up her mind to go where Jesus was walking—not to ask for prayers—but she made up her mind to just touch His clothes!

Consider this, not to touch His hand or His body, which was the common thing to do, but she made up her mind to press through the crowd until she touched the hem of Jesus's garment. There was no indication that she heard anywhere that touching the hem of His garment had any special powers! The idea was crazy and did not make sense. Moreover, Jesus was surrounded by many people who thronged Him. In the natural, there was no way to reach to Him. Jesus was moving with the multitude, and the woman was weak with blood flowing out of her for twelve years.

The breakthrough to her healing started in her mind while she was still in her house. This faith was triggered by a word she heard that Jesus was passing nearby. I believe she said to herself, "This is the day to take action for my miracle. I will arise and go, push through the crowd, push through His disciples until I touch His garment. Once I touch the hem, I will be made whole." (Mark 5:25-28.) Can you imagine what she had to go through?

I imagine people tried to stop her or push her not to advance forward. Maybe she fell a couple of times, but she did not give up. In her mind she kept saying, "I have to be healed today." Read this story. Verse 30 of the same chapter says, "And Jesus, immediately knowing in himself that virtue had gone out of him turned...and said, 'Who touched my clothes?'" His disciples, who we think ought to have known Jesus better, thought He was not making sense by asking such a question, and they did not want Him to stop because they were going to minister to a very important leader in the community. They did not want some unknown, poor person to disturb their important mission. Maybe Peter said, "Jesus, do not embarrass yourself by asking who touched you, because it does not make sense. Since Jairus came to call you to go to his house, many people want to go because he is an important person. Do you not notice how they have been pushing and touching you all along?" Jesus did not pay any attention to what His disciples were saying, or to the rebuke of Peter. He focused on looking around to find a person who had a different touch that was filled with purpose.

Child of God, when you feel in your spirit God is leading you to do something in order to get your breakthrough, depend on Him to bring it to pass, regardless of what it is or how long it takes. Also, it does not matter how many people might seem to know how God works tell you otherwise. God is omnipotent, omniscience, and omnipresent. No one can fully know or understand all His ways! You have to be open to the leading of His Holy Spirit to guide you each day of your life through His Word. By faith you have to obey and take action according of what He has spoken to you.

Indeed, in this story, Mark 5:21-24, many people, including His disciples, were walking and touching Jesus like they had done many other times before, without any specific purpose in their mind. But this woman came with a purpose to be healed and she received more than physical healing; she was made whole (Mark 5:31-34). This is a lesson for us to learn. We can be in the presence of God and remain the same. We can be faithful to do all that is required of us in our churches or in our walk with God, but if we do not cultivate that personal sensitivity to what God is saying to us or desire to hear Him take us to another level, in most cases, our spiritual lives will be only routine.

Daily we have to desire a deeper intimate rela-tionship in order to enjoy all His benefits. Face each new day with a knowing that we will totally depend on God who daily loads us with His benefits (Psalm 68:19). Remind yourself to say this simple but powerful truth: This is the day that the Lord has made. I will purpose to rejoice and be glad in it. He is your Father who controls the day; therefore, anticipate the best even if you know you are going to court or to the hospital, etc.

Luke 5:17-26 tells us about a day when Jesus was teaching a nationwide leadership conference. The power of God was present to heal them, but they were occupied with their titles, positions, even their service to Him; they missed their breakthroughs. They were there with Him but did not realize that the needs they had, God was able to solve them. In fact, whatever they needed, Jesus was able to provide, but they missed it until four men came with a sick friend. These men were not even inside the conference; they were outsiders who were able to receive a miracle. It is a sad story because those who were listening to Jesus were familiar with Him and did not tap into His anointing. Nor did they allow other people who were in need to approach Him. Those carrying a sick friend tried to go through the door, a normal way of entering a house, but the door was blocked by people who were listening to Jesus, and no usher on duty allowed them in. I can imagine what they said: "Sorry, you are late. All the leaders are listening to him, and he cannot be disturbed. Maybe tomorrow; make an appointment or come two hours early to see him." Thank God for those friends who refused to be discouraged. They were focused with one think—to take their friend in the presence of Jesus—and nothing could stop them.

When your day has come, nothing can stop what God has purposed to do in and with you. In fact, you have been told that every day is loaded with your blessings and miracles. In order to receive them, you must anticipate and do the unthinkable. Your determined goal is achievable if you make up your mind like these four friends. When no one allowed them to take their sick friend to where Jesus was, they went on top of the conference hall/house and they started breaking the roof. Surprisingly, no one came to stop them. Even when they interrupted the meeting and lowered their friend before Jesus, they did not receive any rebuke but praise for their unstoppable faith (Luke 5:17-25.)

As a child of God, whatever you do in order to reach your destiny, to achieve your goals or to improve your life and the life of others for God's glory, be sure there will be obstacles and hindrances from different people or circumstances to delay you. Do not be discouraged; God will back you up. He will cause what seems impossible, crazy, or rude in the sight of others to produce your desired goal or miracle. He is your Father who will never leave you if you take a step of faith.

When young David heard the words of defiance from the giant and saw Israel's army running away in fear, he decided to take action. He did not call a committee or a prayer meeting. He did not even ask permission from his brothers or run to tell his father what he was planning to do. To make matters worse, fighting was not part of his training or agenda; he was sent by his father to deliver food.

A man or woman who spends intimate time with God knows when opportunity arises. The army saw Goliath as a big problem, but the boy David, who was not regarded to do anything significant except look after his father's sheep, saw an opportunity to kill Goliath and let God be glorified. David said, "Who is this uncircumcised Philistine, that he should defy the armies of the living God?" (1 Samuel 17:17-31).

As you continue reading the story, you will see how David withstood opposition. His brothers rebuked him for coming to the warfront; no one took David seriously when he said he would kill Goliath. I am sure some of them said, "Boy, who do you think you are? You have no experience *in war*." The more they talked about how he could not kill the giant, the more David continued to speak the death of Goliath. He did not pay attention to their criticism or their advice to stop what he was saying. Some of the soldiers went and told King Saul about the rude boy who was saying crazy things. The king told them to bring the boy to him. Can you imagine what went on in their minds? I am sure they thought that they had him—David would fear the king and, for sure, he would change his mind and go back home, where he belonged.

How many people have been discouraged because a situation seemed impossible? When they tried to take action to solve whatever was happening and make their lives better, they were criticized, their idea dismissed as nonsense, at times called proud if they insisted; no one supported or encouraged them. If you are facing a similar discouragement because no one backs you up, don't give up. (David's brothers did not support him, but that didn't stop him! The woman with an issue of blood, no one was able to stop her from receiving her miracle. The four friends broke the law by entering through the roof because they were not discouraged by the crowd that did not allow them to pass through the normal channel. All these examples should inspire you to overcome any situation that has hindered you.) Put your hope in God. Do not let anyone stop what you know God has called you to do. Do not give up anticipating a breakthrough in your life, in the life of your children or family. No matter how long it takes, it will come to pass because God has not forgotten you.

ANOTHER LESSON

We can learn a lot from how David thought and spoke. As soon as he was before King Saul, David said, "Let no man's heart fail because of him; your servant will go and fight with this Philistine" (1 Samuel 17:32). David was not afraid to start speaking confidently with the king. He broke all human protocol because he knew he represented the King of kings and the Creator—his God and your Father. No matter how King Saul tried to convince the boy not to fight Goliath, David knew who he was and whose he was. He did not depend on the natural signs to have victory; he depended on the power of his God, who never forgot him when he faced other challenges, like the lion and the bear.

I encourage you to read the entire story; you will understand the opposition David faced. His elder brother Eliab was angry to see David speaking with the soldiers concerning the reward of the man who would kill Goliath. Eliab accused David of being proud and haughty in his heart. He spoke aloud in anger for all the other soldiers to hear how his young brother was irresponsible by leaving his sheep and coming to see the battle. David could have become embarrassed and given up. It hurts more when your own family, friends, coworker, or your church discredits you. David paid no any attention to his brother's accusations; he did not want to be distracted. Do not pay attention to those who want to frustrate your efforts to change and succeed.

The woman we read about in Luke 5:25-34 was not always sick. According to the story, she must have been a well-to-do woman in her community. However, circumstances caused her to spend all her life savings paying medical bills. Instead of getting better, she grew worse until she was left alone. When she heard Jesus passing, no one took her to Jesus. Alone she decided to go. The good news is this: in her twelve years of suffering, she was never forgotten, God was watching over her; that is why she was alive to hear that Jesus was passing by. Today, you are reading this book because God has a good, divine purpose for you. Take a moment to think the times you might have been destroyed or wanted to give up, but somehow you are still here because God has not forgotten your purpose for creating you. You are special. You need to encourage yourself that you will make it. You will overcome and your future is bright because God is watching over you.

At the same time, I am sure many have given up or did not accomplish what God wanted them to do because they were not supported by others—especially those who were leaders or who were more experienced than they were. Also, many opportunities have been missed by individuals as well as the Body of Christ because of programs and protocols that are the norm. David heard and saw the problem, but he did not wait to discuss it with the team or the king. Instead, I believe he talked within himself. I imagine in his heart, mind and soul he talked with God and received assurance that he was not alone. He used what was familiar to him to solve a problem the qualified army could not solve.

After that inner assurance, David decided to solve the problem without approval of his family or king. He had seen and saw Goliath killed before it was manifested. The woman with an issue of blood, she spoke being healed before it was manifested. This is how children of God are expected to live and handle different situations in their lives. They need to learn to speak those things that are not as though they are because they know that is the language of their loving Father. When they speak His language, He will hear and help in their every need. Even if the answer does not come according to how we want, still God is working out His plan for our good. His timing of doing things for His children is perfect.

REALITY CHECK

We are in the last of the last days. This book is to help God's children take stock of their lives in order to move from glory to glory. Let us have a reality check on our lives. Can you honestly say you are fulfilling what you were born to do, or is your life just routine? Maybe you are caught up with doing or supporting the norm and what is popular, and you are tired and frustrated. You feel there is more to life, but you do not know what to do. Do not give up; God is waiting for you to turn to Him and talk with Him intimately, not ritualistically or religiously, but relationally. I guarantee He will direct you.

There are many people who do not know God as their Father; there are so many others who are in a valley of decision and are looking for someone to reach to them and make their lives meaningful. If you see yourself in either of these groups, it is not too late. God wants you to surrender to Him; take a step to do what is not popular and decide within yourself to build an intimate relationship with Him. You will know God as your Father, and your life will start to have meaning; you will be fulfilled.

I pray for more Christians to be involved in doing what is not common. Learn to enjoy praying by themselves. Make it a priority to spend more intimate time with God, read His Word every day, and be still before Him. You will hear how He loves you and how He has created you to live victoriously and make an impact for His glory. While others depend on the natural solutions to solve problems, be like David, who said, "You come to me with a sword, and with a spear, and with a shield: but I come to you in the name of the Lord of hosts, the God of the armies of Israel, whom you have defiled" (1 Samuel 17:45). "Some trust in chariots, and some trust in horses: but we will remember the name of the LORD our God" (Psalm 20:7). To remember the name of our Lord is to first share with Him all our problems and concerns. He has all the answers and He can give us ideas on how to solve the problem or give us grace to go through it.

Victory came to the children of Israel because a young boy who was despised dared to step out by faith in the Name of His God. You also can depend on the same name to live above your situations. My life is filled with miracles and uncommon experiences because of my faith walk with God. Unquestionable faith has made me achieve so much and I give God the glory. I remember spring semester of 1981 when I did not have money to register at Oral Roberts

University. By faith I went to talk to the Registrar to enroll me because I did not want to miss classes. The registrar looked at me and laughed, saying aloud for all to hear, "Everyone comes here by faith. You are not the only one. You have to bring money to pay for your classes. No money, no classes! Next," as he pushed my paper aside.

I was embarrassed, but as I left, I started talking directly to my Father. I knew He heard all that went on and I wanted Him to know how I felt. My first time in America, to go to the Oral Roberts University, was a miraculous experience. God took me from Sweden to America supernaturally; however, that is for another book. So when I talked to God, I knew the basis of why I could not miss any class, He had to do something about it quickly; otherwise, He is the one who will be embarrassed and not me.

After two hours, I felt an urge to go to check my campus post office mail. As I opened my box, I found a letter from an unknown person with a $3,000 check as part of my tuition. I ran to the registrar and handed him the check. When he saw it, he said sarcastically, "Now what do we have here? You wanted to hide the money in your dorm and pretend you came here by faith! We know students like you. You think you are smart so you can spend the money!" I looked at him and said, "Sir, yes, I came by faith because my Father said He would educate me. When He intervened at the time I was to take my own life when I thought He had lied to me and I did not want to serve Him anymore. He took me from the mission field to bring me here, and now He has just provided the money for my second semester. Check the campus stamp; then you will know." He looked at the campus stamp that showed the letter arrived at 12:30 p.m. that day. Indeed, God is faithful. From that day, my tuition was miraculously being paid by people I never met. My school gave me different scholarships. While other international students who did not have support were suffering and trying hard to find work to get money, I was busy encouraging and going on mission trips. I am fulfilled when I see people getting saved and Christians living to glorify God.

When you read the end of the chapter about David and Goliath, you see the typical behavior of human beings—unless you prove yourself, you are not important. As soon as David killed Goliath, the king wants to know his name and whose son he was (1 Samuel 55-58). Before, he was just a boy; now he was worthy to be known. Child of God, you are more worthy than what people may give you credit for.

Do not worry about any negative labels you may have been given; do not focus on the negative. Just focus on building your intimate relationship with your Father. He cares for you. He wants to lift you up and He can change your situation in a moment. Do not even pay attention to the tricks of the devil; his intention is to destroy you and to hinder God's purpose in your life. The devil can remind you of your past failures, mistakes, challenges, even obsta-

Never Forgotten

cles. Be encouraged to know that your past does not determine your future. Your future is brighter than what it is right now. You must start to call yourself what you want to be or to name that situation according to what you desire to be. Also, do not forget that you are blessed because you are a child of the most High Living God, who has never forgotten you. You are a carrier of His divine plans and purpose, in your generation and in whatever vocation He has called you to be.

IS THIS POSSIBLE?

God is the One who controls everything, and He wants you to connect to Him in order to enjoy all that He has for you. You might be a carrier of an idea or a dream that will bless many people. Your present situation is temporary. You will arise to fulfill your destiny. Even if you see other Christians who might seem to accomplish much, know that they could not have done so on their own power. They also had to believe in the love of God through Jesus Christ as it is written in Titus 3:3-7. Anyone who has a desire to be used by Him or to see situations change can achieve it. Nevertheless, you have to totally depend on Him. According to His infinite love, your situation can change. God can start to reveal deep and secret things not known to man for a special purpose or task (Daniel 2:22). Maybe you have been struggling because you have an end-time assignment. Maybe you are a person to bring solutions to the ills

91

of the society or community. I will share personal experiences to drive home this point.

God still speaks and directs the affairs of men. I believe July 21, 2007, was an appointed time when God wanted Christians across the United States and the world to unite—on the same day—and make godly declarations. He had been speaking different things for us to pray about since 1994. The call was specifically to Africans, those with ties to Africa, and friends of Africa to unite and, in one accord, declare God's purpose for Africa and America. I called it "Africa for Jesus Continental Prayer and Praise Campaign." I thank God for all who were and still are part of the Africa/America for Jesus (AFJ) Prayer movement. Many who were expected or requested to help run with the 2007 united prayer campaign did not heed the call. Nevertheless, those who participated held prayers and made God's decrees in different parts of the world.

Four of us went to Tanzania, East Africa, for the campaign. On that appointed day, church leaders and government officials united for a declaration march across the city and finished at Biafra grounds. (It would take another book to tell the outcome of that prayer campaign.) I do, however, want to mention an incident that shocked me while I was there during the Continental Prayer and Praise Campaign. After the special meetings were over, I received a phone call from a newly consecrated bishop of the second-largest denomination in Tanzania. This bishop is a highly influential man. His consecration was tele-vised and the whole country watched; people from around the world participated. Bishops from differ-ent denominations and the president of the nation were among the dignitaries at his consecration. He is an influential person in the sight of the world and before God.

When I took the call, the bishop wanted to know how long I would be in Dar es Salaam, the capital city. Before answering, I offered my congratulations on his elevation and the bishopric consecration. He then said, "I would like to see you." (In the back of my mind, I was wondering, *See me for what?*) He continued. "I want you to pray for me before I offi-cially start my duties at the headquarters." When I heard the reason he wanted to see me, I was taken aback, but at the same time it felt better to know why he wanted to see me.

I said, "Sure. Where can I meet you?"

He said, "No, I will come to you. Tell me where you are."

In the natural, that is impossible. Here is a man of God who has been celebrated around the nation who is calling me, an unknown person in the circles of "who's who" in society and in the circle of *so-called "spiritual leaders*," to pray for Him. Though it was a shock to me and a very humbling experience, I knew he had recognized the spirit of God in my life, heard my testimonies, observed my fruits, and wanted to tap into it. The Word says, "Just as iron sharpens iron, friends sharpen the minds of each other" (Proverbs 27:17, CEV).

Even today or when it happened, if others heard that this renowned man called me for prayers, they would not believe it. In fact, when I told my brother, whom I was staying with, he did not believe me. He said, "Nicku, how can you say the big bishop we saw on TV wants to come to see you?" My sister-in-law was busy laughing at the idea. It seemed incredible to them, but I did not want to give any explanation; I just wanted their permission to let the bishop come to their home where I was. My brother agreed, thinking it would not happen. As he left for a meeting, he told his wife to call the office as soon as the bishop came so he could leave the meeting and return home to see him. When my sister-in-law told me what her husband said, I told her to let him know we would not stop the prayers when he arrived. If he found us praying, we would finish before we did the formal introduction. Culturally, it is not polite for the owner of the house to come and you carry on with what you are doing without acknowledging him. But when I am ministering, God is above culture, and my brother would have to wait. The bishop came, we prayed, and God was glorified. What did not make sense in the natural was carried out to His glory.

There are things or situations only God knows and reveals for us to take action without understanding all the details. In 2004, I wrote the book called *Get Ready for Change* because I kept hearing God say He wanted the Body of Christ to unite and prepare for change. The focus was for the people of African descent in the United States to pray, unite and prepare for central stage in the world. Since 1993—when God said to claim Africa and America, along with other nations, for Jesus—consistent strategic prayers on every third Saturday of the month have been going on in different locations. This was a call to bring unity to the Body of Christ, and it is the same call today.

Unfortunately, the Body of Christ does not seem to understand the importance of unity if it is given through an ordinary vessel—nor do they care. The Body of Christ is caught up in personalities, forgetting how Christ came! Redemption came through an ordinary, young virgin named Mary. When she shared how Angel Gabriel visited and spoke to her, no one believed Mary. Even in the Old Testament when Joseph, the son of Jacob, shared his dreams with his family, he was hated by his brothers and no one believed in what he was saying (Genesis 37:6–8). God is still speaking in different ways. He is speaking different things to different people to make sure His Body is doing what they are supposed to do and to be ready for His return. However, He is also calling for united prayer that will bring end-time revival. It was in 1993 when Third Day call to pray came. Thank you for all who believe and continue to pray on the "Third Day." According to His divine calculations, we are now living on the Third Day, which is the sign of His return.

Again, in 2005, specific instruction came—the focus was for Christians in America with ties to Africa to start being involved in politics. Since I was not sure how to handle instructions on politics, I called a meeting with some Christian ambassadors, the International Monetary Fund (IMF), bishops, and religious leaders to seek their counsel. After sharing what God had spoken, they all felt it was time to start an organization on that line. We held several meetings under Africa Leadership Forum. In the process, God revealed to me a need for Africans to come together and have a Thanksgiving Rally on the Washington D.C. Mall and showcase Africans or people of African descent who are in politics and professionals who are making different contributions in the United States of America. I started speaking about it and looking for any person in America with ties to Africa who were involved in making an impact in different areas of leadership in American politics.

The ambassadors mentioned several names across the United States and the entire team agreed to invite one senator as a speaker for the rally. I wrote the senator and sent letters to his office on Capitol Hill and his office in Chicago. As we attempted to mobilize different denominational leaders of every group for the rally, the response was disappointing. Most leaders wanted to know who was behind it. When no big name was mentioned, they were not interested. Those in the preparation team kept pushing the responsibility to me. "Dr. Mordi," they said,

"God told you to do it. We are here to support you!" This meant, we are not owning the vision! As time approached, a regret telephone call from the senator came. It was disappointing, but it did not stop me from continuing to find other means to fulfill what God had spoken.

I must admit, preparing a rally at the D.C. Mall requires committed manpower from different professions and lots of money. I did not have the manpower or a budget. Raising funds is not one of my strengths, and no one was willing to work on fundraising or to contribute the money we needed. Nevertheless, we continued to find alternative ways. I called the IMF partner to go with me to Verizon Center to check the cost. I was bold and full of faith to believe God to use a few hundred dollars given by the ministry partners to multiply and cause people to give toward a worthy cause. After all, we had to obey the Lord and do all we could.

Although I expected a big miracle, God had a different idea. On October 21, 2006, instead of holding the rally on the Washington D.C. Mall, or the Verizon Center, we held it at Greater Mount Calvary Holy Church on Rhode Island Avenue in North East D.C. I thank God for Bishop Alfred Owens, who allowed us to use his church for that divine mandate, Bishop Don diXon Williams and all who worked hard and those who participated in the rally. Though the rally was held indoors and not on the Mall as anticipated, though the senator did not come to speak, we were not discouraged because we had carried out our instructions. God does not see people according to their material wealth or how big their names are; rather, He looks at the heart and the motive of what is being done. Though there were not many at the rally, I was content knowing what God had intended was somehow fulfilled. Obeying God when it does not make sense to anyone is what I call "blind faith."

After the October 2006 Thanksgiving prayer rally, intercessory prayer continued every third Saturday as before and so did the mobilizing of leaders for the July 2007 Continental Prayer and Praise Campaign. This was a call for Christians in Africa and in America to unite in prayer and thanksgiving for what God had done and was about to do. Thank Him for many things even for the prayers He had answered and for the power He has given to His Body. I was consumed by it because I knew it was from God! We distributed information everywhere, using various media resources and networking with leaders around the globe. We did not give up, even though many did not pay any attention to our efforts because we were working by faith and not by finances. I am thankful for the leadership team who believed when I said things that were humanly impossible. Many times, the instructions that God gives during intimate moments are hard to be understood or embraced by everyone.

However, one year later, there was a wind of change in American politics like God had been saying. I looked at the logo we would have used during the rally on the D.C. Mall and it all made sense. The logo was a map of Africa inside the map of the USA. Many did not understand, no matter how I tried to explain to them. Their logic was "Africa is far bigger than America"—the logo did not make sense to them, and that was very true; Africa is very huge. Inside you can put India, Europe, China, Argentina, New Zealand, United States and still there will be space remaining. Some were upset with the logo, saying I was minimizing her greatness. I kept telling them it had a spiritual meaning because God had designed it for a specific purpose; they did not want to hear. Most all who heard the explanation did not get it because spiritual things are hard to be understood with natural faculties. Nevertheless, what God had spoken in 2005 for Africans, African Americans who are friends of Africa to be involved in politics started to unfold. Indeed, God does nothing without revealing it to His children.

Senator Barack Obama's announcement shocked many around the world. He was not known by many people, but God knew Him. Memory flushed within me, how God had spoken in 2004! I started telling everyone Obama would be the forty-fourth president even before he started the campaign. My husband thought I was crazy, and others thought I was nuts. It was surprising. Even those who were at the meeting did not want to connect to what was taking place and what I had told them. It did not matter because

God had revealed it to me during our intimate time together. There was no need for me to worry except enjoy the moment to see God fulfill what He had revealed. Also, it was up to me to choose whom to believe; I decided to believe God rather than anyone else or to observe the historical fact of how impossible it was, because nothing is impossible with God.

In the middle of the election campaign, I told my husband that Obama would be the president and Hilary Clinton would be Secretary of State. My husband and others refused to believe. My children urged me to just pray for him and for his protection because there were some who would want him killed because it was impossible for a black person to become president, "especially Barack Obama! Even his name does not fit the status quo," they argued. It is very discouraging when the people you love the most or those who are close to you are not encouraging no matter what you say; you could easily give up. Because of my intimate time with God, their opinion did not discourage me; I was just laughing when they did not believe. It did not matter because I was the one God had spoken to and I did not need public approval, although it would have been nice. Indeed, the first black president is in the White House in the most powerful country in the world. Imagine for a moment that in 2004 I wrote a book in a few days titled *Get Ready for Change*. Then, in 2005, when I met with Christian ambassadors, religious leaders and IMF leaders, I was not seeking anything except to share what God had said concerning Christians in America with ties to Africa. I had no idea the book was also prophetic because the Democratic theme for Obama was, "Change is here." Does God favor one party over the other? No, God sees what is in the heart and He does what He wills to whom He chooses. Because the foolishness of God is wiser than men, and the weakness of God is stronger than men (1 Corinthians 1:25, NKJV). God has no political party except to desire His children to have dominion over everything and live according to His will that was accomplished by His Son, Jesus Christ.

"God chose...what the world thinks is unimportant and what the world looks down on...God did this so that no one can brag in his presence" (1 Corinthians 1:28-29).

I believe the entire revelation was to awaken Christians, especially church leaders in Africa and America, to unite and be focused to promote God's kingdom and God's agenda for end-time harvest. At the same time, I am convinced that if Christians heard the call from the Africans to come together on the Washington D.C. Mall as God intended, now it would be a different story. I believe God put Barrack Obama as president of this great nation to fulfill His end-time plan, that was to be manifested or not yet revealed but the church missed it and continues to miss the revelation.

We miss opportunities or God's plan are sometimes aborted because we fail to understand fully that

God's ways are not our ways. Many times He might say or direct without making sense to our human minds or way of thinking. At the same time, I feel the church missed because the enemy has blinded us not to see a bigger picture of the Kingdom business and discern the times. Arise, children of God, and take your God-given positions.

Look around you; listen to the events happening around the world. Things are not like before. We are in the last days, and God is looking for those who will trust Him to be vessels of unity to fulfill the last prayer of Jesus in John 17:21-23. I am sorry to say that if we do not repent from our biopsies, things will continue to be worse regardless of our different prayer efforts. I often wonder what would have happened had Christians gathered in thousands and millions to consecrate the ground and the atmosphere before the historic inauguration. *Just Think*!

CONCLUSION

I hope after reading what has been written in this book you can agree that as a child of God you are, indeed, never forgotten and you are special because your Father God loves you just like He loves Jesus. Purpose in your mind, therefore, to develop a relational prayer lifestyle of intimacy with God—having a pure, sincere love for Him—makes a person decision and determination to live beyond the norm. This does not mean there would not be problems and difficulties, but you will live in victory in spite of what you face because you are loved. Love makes you overcome or live above the daily problems.

For a child of God, many incidents are normal, but to others, they are miracles. It would take many books to document my personal experiences, as I have determined to walk and spend time with God. I am a living testimony of taking God at His word. There are things that happen that others see as impossible, but I consider them normal because I know I am God's child who is never forgotten. God is thinking the best for me and for you too.

Throughout history, God has used ordinary people to do extraordinary things. I know God can use you too. Unfortunately these days, when a so-called ordinary person, in their own eyes, speaks, no one cares to activate their faith to believe. Many of us are caught up in titles and outward appearances. We are too blinded to the things of God and His awesomeness to admit that we do not understand all His ways. I have seen many who have missed their breakthrough because they did not believe the words spoken to them through an ordinary vessel in an ordinary way.

It is not always clear or even easy to believe a person who speaks solution and breakthrough concerning difficult situations that have lasted a long time. But if you know the credibility of the person speaking, or the person is titled a prophet, it is easy to receive the message and believe for a breakthrough. Avoid putting God in a box of any kind. He is God.

There are those moments when you know that you know the Father has revealed something. Do not be afraid to speak or act—even if it does not make sense or seems to be beyond the natural. Activate your faith, and believe it will come to pass.

Recently, I went to visit someone who was not feeling well. She knows me and also regards me as a woman of God. After praying for her and pronouncing blessings upon her and her household, I left. A week later, she called and shared how her freezer and refrigerator had been broken for weeks. As soon as I left, a miracle happened, the appliances started working. I did not specifically pray for the freezer and the refrigerator; nor did I even know they were broken. When she knew I was going to visit her, she purposed in her heart to receive a miracle in her household. I did what was natural for me, but our Father performed a miracle according to her faith.

Can you imagine how good life would be if we truly believed that God is in control and He is concerned about our every need? God has us covered. Yes, we say God is in control, but we continue to be afraid and worried. We read the Word, we quote it and pray scriptures, but the result is not in proportion to the effort we put into our prayers. As a child of God, in your private time with Him, learn to speak the language of love with your Father. He is love and He responds to the love language. When you approach Him, do not give Him complaints all the time; give Him pleasure that is what you are created for (Revelation 4:11). "Let us offer the sacrifice of praise to God [continually], that is, the fruit of our lips giving thanks to his name" (Hebrews 13:15).

I wrote how most people spend too much time focused on problem-solving prayers or prayers of binding and casting out demons. Hours, sometimes days, are spent talking to the devil as they cast him out. Let that not be your first priority. Do not focus on bad situations, although there is a little time for it. Your first priority and desire should be to know God through His Word. Learn and develop the art of intimacy with God; let His glory fill you. Your

Father crowned you with glory and honor since you were a baby (Psalm 8:5-6). Desire to experience this and unpleasant things will start to change. You will spend few minutes solving problems and have more time to be in His presence. In prison, Paul and Silas were praising God when a prison breakthrough came (Acts 16:25). The same will happen to you!

Once you know His Word, your personal relationship with Him will be stronger, unmovable, and you will live victoriously. Storms of life will come, but you will be able to overcome them. Like the man who built his house upon the rock; nothing disturbed Him. When you speak, your voice will carry authority to demolish the power of darkness. Even when you meet for the corporate prayers, there will be greater impact and far more effectiveness. Yes, there is a place and there is a time for binding and casting out demons. What I am sharing here is for you to first strengthen your personal prayer life; know how to spend more time praising and loving God with all your heart, soul, mind and strength. Do this, and when forces of evil come your way, you will be able to resist them and experience the peace and joy of a truly intimate relationship with God. This is achievable because the key to be able to resist the devil is for you to submit yourself to God totally (James 4:7).

Every moment you have is precious; use it to adore Him. When you meet for corporate prayers, nothing can stand the presence you are all carrying together. What is more, many people will be attracted to know the God you serve and worship for who He is. Miracles will be part of your every day service and revival will break forth, not by ritualistic methods, but by your sincere, individual hunger to know God and to be intimate with Him. No one will come to church for performances or to show off but to offer God our corporate prayers and worship and to be fed anew with His Word and filled with His Spirit. Indeed, revival will be inevitable if every individual will truly hunger and thirst for a genuine relationship with Him and focus to please Him alone. "Blessed are they which do hunger and thirst after righteousness: for they shall be filled" (Matthew 5:6). Can you for a while, children of God stop focusing on the material things that we need, or praying prayers that focus on solving problems and decide to know Him and His ways?

I believe God has secrets or strategies that He wants to reveal to you in order to bring you solutions to your problems *and* for you to be used to bring God's kingdom on this earth. This is the reason He inspired me to write this book and remind the Body of Christ and you how important you are to God. You are living today because God has never forgotten you. It is up to You to believe you can speak with Him and He will hear you. Take a step of faith to obey and approach Him as your Father. Acknowledge you know Him and He knows you. Jesus said you should enter into the closet and close the door and say, "My Father, who art in heaven, hallowed be thy name." Because Jesus was teaching many He said "Our

Father" but I wanted you to personalize and feel the impact as you say, "My Father, who art in heaven, Hallowed be thy name. Thy kingdom come… (think, when God's kingdom fills your mind, spirit and soul, you will be an instrument to bring His will to others. Now, continue to pray) "Thy will be done in earth, as it is in heaven. Give us this day our daily bread. And forgive us our debts as we forgive our debtors" (Matthew 6:9-13).

These few words alone can make you pray for hours without being tired. You know where your Father resides. Your Father is steadfast, no matter where you are, and you can find Him at His residence called heaven and the address is "Holy Habitation" (Psalm 99:9; Hebrews 12:14). Without holiness, however, no one can see God. You are holy, not in yourself, but through Christ who lives in you. You can boldly enter your Father's presence.

To continue to expound on this prayer is a different book. Although it is called "Our Lord's Prayer," it is in fact our prayer. Jesus was giving us the pattern on how to pray, start by knowing that you have God who is your Father who has not forgotten you. He is Holy and yet He wants to talk with you and share what you are going through.

Another reason I believe God inspired me to write this book is because many of His children are suffering. Some do not think they matter because their situations appear to remain the same, no matter how they pray. God says not to worry about anything and do not be deceived that no one cares. Your Father has not forgotten you. If He still cares for birds in the field, know that He will care for you far much more (Matthew 6:25-26;31-34). Make the moments of praying alone a very special and more enjoyable time—not for problem-solving time but enjoying Him. Be consumed with Him, and He will fill you with Himself. I promise you, instead of just existing, you will start to live differently. What now seems so difficult to bear will not matter anymore. You will know it is part of life and your Father will help you go through because He watches over you always. Let it settle into your mind and into your spirit that you are important and you are never forgotten. Jesus also confirmed by saying, "In the world, ye shall have tribulation: but be of good cheer; I have overcome the world" (John 16:33). Indeed, be of good cheer, God will send help or a solution that you need at the right time.

Much could be written about spending time in the Word—more so on how you think and speak, because these basics are key to victorious living. The Word of God tells us that as a man thinketh in his heart, so is he (Proverbs 23:7), and that Death and life are in the power of the tongue (Proverbs 18:21). But in this book, I wanted to write on something that is so simple and yet so vital. Everyone longs to be loved and wants to be in an intimate relationship with someone. Indeed, it is good to have another human being who you know loves and cares for you. I want to repeat what I said before: in case you do not have one yet or you had one but the relationship was filled with misery and heartache, be encouraged and start to have hope again—you have *someone* who will never ever let you down, nor will He ever forget you. His agape love is pure and amazing.

Remember Matthew 6:9-13 is *your* prayer. Jesus wants you to build your intimate relational prayer life in that pattern and you will never be bored with praying. When you are becoming mature in the relationship with Him, no matter what you face in life, you will know you have someone who loves you more than anyone else. To become intimate with Him is to know how to spend time in your secret place, that is the place where you will be encouraged and inspired. You will always hear Him giving you advice on how to overcome your struggles or how to better succeed in whatever you are doing. This is a place where He can open up to you, tell you things that no one else knows. Then He can assure you not to be afraid to take a step of faith in what He might instruct you to do. Remember, even if you make a mistake or fail, He will never leave you alone. Indeed, you are His child and you will never be forgotten. What a promise!